Loneliness

Anthology – Volume One

Chantelle Lowe

Published by Chantelle Griffin, originally known as Chantelle Lowe, in 2021

Interior layout by Chantelle Lowe

Cover by Chantelle Lowe

Photograph: Seven Mile Beach

Catalogue-in-Publication details available from the National Library of Australia

hardback ISBN: 978-0-6487786-4-6

Also available in paperback
ISBN: 978-0-6487786-3-9

Dedication

In memory of my first cat, Sam, who took advantage when I wrote in the backyard by rolling down the hill without a care. Happily landing on me with his paws outstretched, then running up the hill to start all over again.

Contents

Loneliness

Abandon imagination	1
Accepting lies	2
Accomplishment	3
Adult	4
Again	6
All is lost	8
All is nothing	10
All was lost	11
All my memories	12
All the shame	13
Alone by myself	15
Alone one day	16

Along the edge   17
A piece of knowledge   18
A rarity   19
A reflection   20
Assertiveness   22
A word without thought   24
Barrier   26
Beckoning   27
Betrayal   28
Betray me   30
Breaking   32
Breaking up inside   34
Broken   36
Burden of sadness   39
But one   40
Calling out   41
Cannot go back   42
Casting away   43
Causing   44
Colder than a game   46
Cold stares   48
Confidence   50
Control   52
Corridors   54

Crashing weight   55
Creasing pain   56
Cruel events   57
Crushing emotion   58
Culmination of fear   59
Daughter of mine   60
Declared   62
Decision   63
Determine   64
Dim darkness   65
Do I dare to dream?   66
Do I exist?   68
Dull ache   70
Embedded   72
Faded memory   74
Fallen down   75
Fall short   76
False hope   77
Far away   78
Figure it out   79
Forever alone   80
For the night   82
For one   83
Fragile structure   84

Fragile thought   86
Frame of mind   88
Framework   89
Frustration   90
Get rid of this feeling   91
Given hope   92
Gone   94
Grip of corrosion   96
Hard to see the light   98
Havoc   99
Heavy on the mind   100
Hiding   101
Hiding away   102
Highest hope   104
Hold on to   105
Holding myself up   106
Holding tight   108
Hopeless   109
Human   110
Hurt   111
I am not afraid   112
I cry   114
Ignored   115
I hold my solitude   116

Inability to interact   117
In a girl's heart   118
Incomprehensible   119
Indifferent tide   120
In dismay   122
In every direction   124
Inner strength   126
In reality   127
I run away   128
Internal pressure   130
In time   132
Into a dream   134
Into nothing   136
Inspiration   138
Invisible   140
Irreplaceable   142
It has meaning   143
I will remain   144
Judgement   146
Left alone   148
Let me be myself   150
Letting go   151
Life   152
Lifting my head   153

Little voice	154
Loneliness	156
Lonely inside	158
Lost dreams	160
Lost within	162
Manifesting	163
Manipulate	164
Maze of deception	165
Mend the soul	166
Mistaken	168
My curse	169
My path	170
Myself	173
My thought flows	174
Needed to know	175
No longer needed	176
No one hears	177
No one helped	178
No one speaks	179
No other	180
No patience	181
No possible way	182
Not for me	185
No time	186

Not my home	187
Not near me	188
Not so sure	189
Not to bother	190
Not yours	191
Not yours to claim	192
No warmth	194
No way out	195
Old owl	196
One of them	198
One so dark	200
One step away	202
On the edge	205
Open to nothing	206
Overwhelming	207
Part of me	208
Passed me by	209
Patience	210
Patiently	211
People that go by	212
Prerequisite	214
Prison of time	216
Proclamation	218
Quietly	220

Reaching forward   222
Reach out my hand   224
Reappear   226
Relief   227
Run from fate   228
Safe place   229
Same situation   230
Say my piece   232
Scar   234
Searching   238
Secret child   239
Sense of being   240
Sharpness   241
Small request   242
So close   243
So deep   244
Solace   245
Spirit   247
Still nothing   248
Suffer the same   249
Suggestions   250
Sure of   251
Tainted minds   252
Talent   253

Take away calm   254
Taken are my dreams   255
The coldest day   256
The only person   258
The quiet   259
The way I cry   260
Through desolation   262
Through the open window   263
Time of attitudes   264
Time makes no sense   265
To be   266
To be complete   267
To be trapped   268
Too close   270
Topple over   272
To reach out   274
Torn between two worlds   276
To think   279
To turn   280
To wake up   282
Toward uncertainty   284
To write   286
Transfixation   287
Treasured thought   288

Two trees   289
Unattainable   290
Uncertainty   291
Underlying tone   292
Underneath the stains   293
Voice   294
Wanting to disappear   298
Went unnoticed   300
What I had   301
What to become   302
What was   303
When all is lost   304
Where nothing is real   308
Who I am   310
Wildest dreams   311
With a threat   312
Without   313
World of expectation   314
Worthless   316

Chantelle Lowe

Photographs

Photographs of Seven Mile Beach,
16 January 2021

Beach	Sand	219
7	121	Shore
14	131	223
21	135	231
29	139	246
38	147	261
45	155	269
51	159	273
67	172	281
71	184	297
95	199	307
113	215	

Acknowledgements

I would like to thank Greg Lowe and Sally Shaw for their encouragement.

Foreward

An old lady pulled out her vehicle, blocking the road and I angled my car to the middle. There was no space, no distance to brake, only silence. I missed the vehicle coming the other way and stopped parallel with the old lady. There was only an inch between our vehicles and I peered straight into her eyes. She was not wearing a seat belt.

It was then that my passenger spoke, 'I had faith in you'.

Chantelle Lowe

Abandon imagination

If you were to abandon the hope,
abandon all reason,
and live up to what others expect,
there would be no thought,
no pride,
no individual imagination.

We would all be dead,
dead of ideas,
dead of hope,
dead of optimism.

And there would be nothing left,
but the husk, the shell,
supposed to support life.

but only animating it.

1

Accepting lies

I have to live with my pain alone,
in a world where others made up a false
past for me.
A past which was not my own.
It means that even if I wanted to,
I cannot enter their world,
because it would mean accepting their lies.
That would be a tragedy in itself,
because it means that I would have to die inside.
It means they do not accept me for who I really am,
It means they do not want to get to know me.
That is the part that really hurts,
after everything I have been through,
they do not value me for who I am.

Chantelle Lowe

Accomplishment

I've done it
I have accomplished everything.
What am I,
When I am here?
I do not see this place
as it was.
I do not see
the way I did,
here I am
in a place
I know not where.
Am I to destroy everything,
when everything is nothing?
What am I
When I am here?
Did I come to this
on my own?

Adult

I am one,
I am the child that dies in the night.
I can see you,
reach for me.
Kill my heart and soul,
but leave my spirit behind,
forever may it roam with me.
For I am the child that cries,
where no one hears,
and I am the child you held,
once, long ago.
I am your thought,
but I am my reason.
I carry your will,
but I have my own decision.
I am the child left to die,
and crumble in the storm.
I am the virtue,
of my past,
I am the holder and the destroyer.

Chantelle Lowe

I am the child who has died in your arms,
I am the non-believer,
the hope that never saw yourself.
I am the one side of your past,
you never shared.
I am the child who died many years before,
in the cold night air,
in the strength of silence,
and the stars above.
I am the child that died to the world outside,
I am the child that grew,
from the ice of my past.
I am the child, that bears the heavy weight,
when you look out of your stressful world.
I am the child that can see farther ahead,
I am the child that died.

Chantelle Lowe

Again

Here I am again,
into the all consuming past.
I have been here before,
it remembers me.

All is lost

Give me hope beyond hope,
give me reason beyond reason.
Tell me to look the other way,
and I will,
but what will it achieve?
When all is gone, all is lost,
and everything has been taken.
Stripped of its entirety,
and left to wonder alone,
But will it hold back?
When all is gone,
and the only thing left,
is an arrogance, so overwhelming.
With nothing more for it to do,
nothing left for it to hold.
Nothing to remember,
yet it lives on.

Chantelle Lowe

Killing those around it,
slowly, inevitably,
then dining on itself,
for itself alone.

All is nothing

No hope holds the dawn of tomorrow,
I can find no way out.
All is as nothing,
when no one is seen.
Can nothing be apart,
when no one hears.

All my memories

When I was out and about one time,
I found a little hole,
I knelt down,
and peered through.
I saw my face,
In my eyes, where they were black,
I saw all my thoughts,
and all my memories.
So clear were they,
that I cried,
it blurred my vision,
but it could not ease my pain.

Chantelle Lowe

All the shame

To see what has been wrought,
in all that has begun.
Into this little world,
of all the molten shame.

Chantelle Lowe

All vvas lost

A time when all was lost, and I knew I had to be me.
It was given as a place, a guide to follow,
when little faith was there I stood,
amidst it and watched before all is gone.
I created the space which consumed,
I wanted to know all that was,
even though I was there.

Chantelle Lowe

Alone by myself

The mind wanders, not knowing where to find everyone,
my mind wanders in that direction,
It has been there many times before.
I pondered upon this idea for a while,
as I was alone by myself.
It hurt me to know that I was alone,
but this was something that I had been used to.

Chantelle Lowe

Alone one day

If I were alone one day,
I would say to myself
what are you?
Somewhere deep down inside
I would probably know.

Chantelle Lowe

Along the edge

In this way I want to be, covered in all this sadness.
Is this the way ahead for me, trampled in dismay.
Ever am I seeking kindness, wonderful as it can be.
For this reason I wander away, thinking of what I really am.
This truth which pre-exists my time, colours my world a little.
Though in all hope it is me who follows, when called on from above.
Time did not bring me here without reason,
though I am sure there is some.
Calling from the grave in desperation, hoping for repeal,
but here I am in the midst of this, trying to recall.
The way above is hindered as I walk along its edge,
it calls me from below, hoping to lure me in,
and here I am tormented with these paths I see around.
For all I wanted was safe and simple, but no where to be found.

Chantelle Lowe

A piece of knowledge

I needed to know something and I found it,
a small, little piece of knowledge.
It meant a lot to me,
to have this use.

Chantelle Lowe

A rarity

In a hideaway,
the light is rare,
rarer than a stream of softness,
but nothing,
nothing is forever,
and I am one,
I am one of those,
a rarity.
Making one small finger print,
on the wide span of earth,
then,
never again
to be seen.

A reflection

What do you see in the mirror,
but the reflection of your past,
falling in upon yourself.

Assertiveness

To become alive with fear,
to feel it through your veins.
to know it, to see it.
Discussing the inevitable,
tragic,
Yet it was always that way,
being chastised for being kind,
being hurt for being tolerant,
Being trodden into the ground for being polite.
Being overlooked for being nice.
When I should have been assertive,
when I should have demanded equality.
when I should have made it clear without a doubt.
Being courteous does not always command respect,
it can often lead to being trampled on.
This idea of being polite and showing fear,
are not desirable,

when they lead to nasty outcomes,
one should only show respect when it is due,
not when the person looks down on you,
and automatically writes you off as insignificant and
nothing.
Assertiveness should be shown,
especially for basic rights and basic needs being met.
One must be assertive,
one must command respect,
one must not show the crippled attitude
to be less than equal.
I must command respect.

A word without thought

A past to tear me apart,
a future to guide my hand.
A word without thought,
amidst words with meaning.
Can unravel an entire destiny,
and bring down the harshest truth.
It poisons pure water,
and makes the truth a lie.
It crumbles purity,
and gives fuel to the wicked.
It destroys the innocent,
and gives power to the uncaring.
It takes away rights,
and gives undue privileges.
It turns the tainted into monsters,
and brings the true into harm.
It can take away everything,

and leave a shadow of what was.
A word without thought,
can hurt so greatly.
It can give no rest,
to those who care.
To those who believe,
and know.
Truth shatters,
in the space between the lies.
It cannot sustain what is not,
and it cannot hold its own.
A word without thought,
can be the greatest lie.
It can demolish all else
and leave only pain.

To break the ice,
when it is frozen solid.
It would be easier,
for the ice to break you,
but you must never let it.

Beckoning

A place which finds me,
calls to me.
Beckons me.
Takes me away
and hides me.
A place unknown,
yet known.
A place which reaches forth
and embraces.
Calls out to me,
calls me by name.
Completes the lost unbroken sentence.
Travels forth,
not knowing.
finding me,
in insanity.

Betrayal

Loyalty draped in ugliness,
betrayal.
Oh!
How I have been betrayed.
It deepens my soul,
further and further down,
down to the darkest well I can find.
Have to come out,
must come out.
must go higher,
not lower.
Must deem myself worthy,
of myself.

Betray me

Why! Why do you betray me with your whimpering smile,
cower over me like the shadow of destiny's supposed peace.
How could you call yourself the enchanter, the holder of legend,
your peace does not exist within me,
your ideas are not mine to have or own.
This obliteration you call patience is yours to surround you.
I do not need your religion, I do not need your thought,
I do not need your self-esteem.
I am a person, a living being, I can think for myself.
You do not possess me, you do not grant me your wisdom.
I hold myself high above your serenity,
I do not need your meanings they are useless to me.
They are your abode not mine and not yours to give.
You are not me, you do not know me, you cannot understand what is me.
You do not obliterate me, you will not hold me to your whim.
You who thinks is the idealistic thinks no more.
I am here, I will always be what I am, what is me.

Chantelle Lowe

You cannot hold this.
You cannot imagine that you are holding this.
I cannot let you destroy what I have, what keeps me here.
You will never have it, you will never hold it,
you will never take it.
You who think you are what you possibly can do,
is no more,
and I will exhibit it for all to see,
and you shall wear the humiliation of your downfall.

Breaking

Not everybody sees,
not everybody hears.
Not everybody walks away and hides.
It kills the spirit,
it kills the soul,
it kills not only you and me,
but something deeper,
far deeper.
I have hurt the soul.
I have hurt the spirit.
It calls out to me,
and breaks,
shatters through me,
and past me.
I can feel the shards,
cut,
and slice,

Chantelle Lowe

and bend,
then heal,
into place.

Breaking up inside

Who are these people that I see,
who are these people that speak to me,
in my hour of need.
Who are they, that enter my head,
and give me weird thoughts?
What is this,
that I have to deal with
everyday of my life.
What am I,
when no one else is the same?
What am I supposed to do,
when I cannot see any more?
When the road ahead,
has not come to me yet.
What am I supposed to do,
when I am breaking up inside?
This is not the way it was supposed to be,

Chantelle Lowe

this was not what I had thought about me.

Broken

It's gone,
it's shattered,
into tiny little pieces.
If you glue it back together,
it will never be the same.
No matter how much you try,
it will never be achieved,
never.

All hope is lost,
vanished, nowhere to be seen.
You can't understand it,
why it is happening,
you can't stop it,
you can't intervene.
It is between other people,
but it affects you just as bad,

but nothing can be done about it,
nothing.

You try to steady yourself,
amongst the shattered pieces.
No matter how much you try,
it cuts you,
makes you bleed.
You hurt,
your agony,
suffered by all.
You can't do anything about it,
can't.

Burden of sadness

One day, when sunlight touches the eaves
and swings over the dampened glass,
a light with warmth and sadness which touches my soul.
Colours my day with different feelings over what has been,
I did as much as I could and more, but yet that was not enough.
A lot of energy came to nought in front of me,
and I was left with such an overwhelming sensation
of being on the outside.
A lost soul wandering alone, not really belonging any where,
with such a great feeling of sadness ringing through me.
I find myself at a loss, a great deep, deadening loss,
taking away all my effort, all my hard work, everything I created.
Can such pain and sorrow be real when it takes such a burden,
when the whole dream was left shattered and nothing could be repaired.
It is not known by the world how such a toll has affected me,
a hollowness inside, a deep extraction from society,
a society I tried so hard to be a part of.

But one

I am but one person.
What does one person
know about all the problems
of the world?
Very little.

Chantelle Lowe

Calling out

I hear myself calling, calling out,
it hurts my head and I cry,
it is not the pain that makes me cry.
It is the reason behind it,
that hurts my head and deepens my sadness.
I can die, I want to die,
that is the pain that I feel,
in my head.

Cannot go back

So what do I do, what do I do now,
after all this is finished, and crumbled.
I can't go back, I know that, all too well,
unfortunately.

Cast away

I have had strange thoughts run through my head,
and I do not know what to do with them.
They cast away my ideas
and give me a lot to despise.
It is the way they look at me
and see me as nothing more.
I live in a world
where people assume that I am untrustworthy,
They write me off before giving me a chance.
I know that I am different,
sometimes I feel more different than others.
What did I do to live like this?
I do not understand.

Causing

I am going to face a side
of my past I cannot explain.
I find it so harsh
it causes me pain.

Colder than a game

The voice called,
down the winding alleyway,
follow me, follow me.
I turned my head and there it was,
colder than the mind's evil games.
It stared its cold eyes into mine,
this was not a game,
and I knew it.
Across, I heard the children playing,
their innocence could be felt in myself.
I was not yet ready to give up,
it taunted me with its words.
I held myself,
I would not let go.
I WOULD NOT LET GO!
I thought it was too late,
but it was not.

Chantelle Lowe

I opened my eyes,
and for the first time I could see.

Cold stares

The world and all its fun passes me by,
people just pass me by.
They dislike me, or they exclude me,
and I am left alone.
All I have to comfort me,
are my own thoughts,
and they are not so pleasant.
I want to get out of this place,
I want to leave it all behind,
I want to escape and be free.
I do not want those horrid people,
with their excluding stares.
I do not want their clicking tongues,
which keep me on the outside.
I just want to be me,
to be able to express myself,
away from all those cold stares,

Chantelle Lowe

and degrading remarks.
I want to let them go without a care,
and show them that it does not bother me,
and that I will move on.

Confidence

I stand here willingly,
no face to force me,
no others expressions,
no others ideas.
All are and will ever be my own.
Look around me,
you see others,
comes with that,
others opinions,
make you think twice,
make you change your mind.
Force you,
shape you,
your ideas,
mix,
smothered.

Control

Life is cruel, it hides unseen.
It calls to me, it wanted me to be weighed down.
When I flew it cried.
Unseen tears of immortal shame gathering speed,
increasing down the long slope of intrigue.
What have I done?
When I turned away I saw nothing,
I cried so deep. My control was imperfect,
and I knew it would not be long,
before I saw the reason for abstention.
I wanted so badly to be one at peace,
I wanted to fight so hard for a reality.
I fought time and time again,
I wanted it even more than I wanted life,
then it broke me down, it cowered over my soul,
and it denied my very existence.
It left me, even though I knew I had left it.

Chantelle Lowe

It wanted something I did not possess,
control.

Corridors

Mad,
Maybe?
I just walk the corridors of life,
and open them.

Chantelle Lowe

Crashing weight

As spindles, spindles,
tall and brown,
in ever dark come,
crashing down,
I feel the weight,
as one would hope.

Creasing pain

Pain, the immortal sin.
Creasing through my body, shivering up my spine.
It takes hold of my form, toying with me playfully,
but this is not a game.
Cold is all I feel in my lower chest, artificial and harsh,
raking up past my lungs.
I am still mobile and clear of my head,
but my lower abdomen sends pain winding through hidden tunnels,
and my chest gives in, letting it seep higher.
A radius covers the area like a ground zero,
flattening all in its path.
I shed tears, it is not immense but it comes and goes,
and it is enough to be unbearable.
I didn't want this, it sends shivers down the tops of my arms.
All I want is for it to end, but it hangs on,
as though taunting me.

Chantelle Lowe

Cruel events

How do I know my own mind?
When I do not know myself.
My individuality seems to escape me,
hiding around the corner of my eye.
I begun this journey long ago,
set on this path by cruel events.
Given misery and shame,
then picked out and blamed,
with the conviction that only comes from lies.
I want to find myself,
escape the old drudgery,
left behind by hatred.

Crushing emotion

The soul is hurt too deep,
the cut seeps emotion and no other.
Taking in the current, the sounds to weep,
and somehow no one seems to bother.
I could have, yet I could not, the door was closed before I looked,
and opened by others without me.
I do not know if it was meant to be that way,
should I be surprised when it has happened before?
I lay my head down in my hands and wonder what I did,
when I know the answer is nothing just the same.
The crushing blow that made me hid,
from the taunts and vexations of someone else's game.
The parody that takes over when I have no escape,
a clamour of thoughts which take away with one effort,
A person's stray and happy beginnings,
and turns them into mud.

Chantelle Lowe

Culmination of fear

Culmination of fear, degradation,
evolving, taking time.
Rejection, not knowing.
Take, take away.

Daughter of mine

Oh daughter of mine,
turn away from the border,
the one who longs for you is there.
It is the ghost calling out to your soul,
you have to go now.
You mustn't,
it will tear everything you have done,
and turn it into ashes.
Your gift is more important than that,
look for it inside you,
you will find it nowhere else.
Please keep it safe,
it is precious,
do not let it have what is yours by right,
otherwise no one will know what it was,
what you could have done.
Do not give way, it is always there as a choice,

only a choice.
Do not let it eat you,
destroy what you have.
Your gift is the most important thing to you,
and to others,
do not let it die so quickly.
It is just beginning to show,
your importance will serve you well.
Let it live,
let it thrive,
you have it in you.
Let your gift show, raw and beautiful,
please don't let it waste.
It is too thick in your blood,
let it show.

Declared

If I knew what it really was,
would I declare it?
An image so hideous,
it extends to the extreme.
Replicating evil,
cruelty beyond belief.
Do I live a lie,
when I see the truth?
I chose the implications of being true.
I took hold in my hand the responsibility that went with it.
I declared what had been fact.
Most importantly,
I did not lie to myself.

Decision

My life has been so seriously damaged,
yet again I am ploughed into the ground by those who wield power
and influence.
Using it to come crushing down, shattering dreams,
throwing away so much hard work, so much effort.
All I could do was accept a decision I had no control over,
a decision that came from power, from intolerance,
from lack of understanding.
All I could do was accept a decision I had no control over,
fall onto my small and fragile shoulders, to weigh me down so low.
A weight so heavy it hides some of the shock that flowed from knowing,
a decision which cost so much more than anything I could have imagined.

Determine

Placement of the key in position,
claiming of ones' own.
Dispelling myth, creating legend.
Reasoning with time.
Killing the soul, or making it mine.

Chantelle Lowe

Dim darkness

When all fall down we reach for the skies,
yet what do we see at the other side.
For the path is crippled ahead,
and no one can change that.
The other path is so long ahead,
and I do not see a beginning.
All I see is the dim darkness,
reaching forward,
And I wonder what it is for,
when all I want to do is leave.

Chantelle Lowe

Do I dare to dream?

There is no time to change the present, when the past is so extreme,
in this place I call my own do I dare to dream?
The light glows down on the grass below,
dreading what is to follow.
Yet unseen shall remain everything,
when all of this caves to nothing.

Chantelle Lowe

(Do I exist?)

Do I exist?
Yes I do exist,
to the unknown face of time.
I call,
I know not what.
For calling out can bring pain.
I am a time, a space,
a nothing,
To call upon indignantly.
I am the separation,
of a whole,
The obliteration of destiny.
Come!
Why don't you come when I call?
What have I done,
that you haven't?
In time, and space,

and nothing,
I am the configuration,
to who I am.
Call!
Call to it as what,
a name?
I am who you are,
what is different?
To see myself,
I see no one else,
but I do see a complex beauty,
of the images calling out.
Am I lost,
lost to desperation?
No, here I stand,
with me alone.

Dull ache

Time takes away the hand of trust,
and leaves a rhythm of pain.
Thriving in a dull ache.
No one knows where,
when time grips the enemy.
Placement of insanity, calling forth.
Frothing on the foam of sequential behaviour.
What is this?
The autonomy?
Reaper is calling from a distance.
Enemy of mine.
Reckless creeper of maniacal joy.
Cataclysm of jealousy is seen in the eye
that awaits disturbance.
Pretending to be.

Embedded

Insanity comes calling from both sides,
playing at my finger tips.
Taking the strength from my soul,
whispering the past in my ears.
Calling from another time,
when hope had faded into insignificance.
I remembered more than perhaps I should have,
it was from a time when I knew little of the world.
I had been trapped by past incidents,
into a harsh and uncaring atmosphere.
I was too scared, even though I wanted to leave,
I was frightened of hurt in this place.
Pain reached me where I was and soon became too much,
I was not able to deal with it, I was too young.
It pulled at my reality,
and embedded itself in me.
I tried to remove it by harming things important to me,

Chantelle Lowe

I tried to remove it by causing myself pain.
Always it has remained a part of me, not really leaving,
I want to do something about it, but I don't know if I can,
it feels as though I am living this way for the rest of my life.

Chantelle Lowe

Faded memory

Kill not me,
forsaken my soul,
carry on dear memory,
for I haven't got long.
See my patience rise,
colour me down,
see my harm is not broken.
For the fading ice is melting,
and when my waken body,
flies through the flames of fire,
I see at the end of the light,
my mind shall come to rest,
though my memory shall stand strong.

Chantelle Lowe

Fallen down

All my dreams have died away
and my soul is not yet free.
In this world that's wrapped around
and the sadness I can see.
From the sky that's fallen down,
comes the dark taking a hold,
in the breeze that grew so cold.

In my hand I see the way,
it's so vague and hard to find.
In amidst the slow decay,
crossing paths over the mind.
Up ahead I cannot see,
a clear way to destiny.

I fall short

Is what I see now.
How can I keep track of time,
when it escapes me.
I see the world as an inescapable challenge,
eroding my esteem for honesty.
When I see the workings of the corrupt,
in place to protect themselves.
I do whatever I can,
yet I still manage to fall short.
Is this the world
which accepts all for who they are?

Chantelle Lowe

False hope

The false hope caressing my soul,
torments my ever fragile mind.
In this warring world of society,
I was given something so false.
The evil flowing from its web,
incarcerated my being,
and left me knowing,
that it is here for eternity.
Here I have run to find,
that even though I am free,
this insidious being still exists,
and corrupts my dreams.

Far away

Go away insanity,
come back again another day.
I don't want you here,
I don't want anybody.
I just want to be left in peace.
I want to go away,
to some other place,
far away.
I just want to be me.

Figure it out

A life unknowing, uncaring.
A life I am still trying to figure out.
One which I was given,
one which I do not understand.
Is this life?
I am not aware of the outcome.
One where I am not aware of what
I am supposed to be.

Forever alone

I was thrust on the heap without a second look.
Passing by without a hesitation, keeping me on the outside,
always keeping me there.
Keeping me there and not wanting me.
How do I move forward, how do I break out?
All around the world seems impossible.
It saddens and upsets me,
am I really bad, remaining undiscovered.
Remaining forever on the outside.
I am unique, from a unique past,
and I cross each hurtle respectively, but I am forever alone.
Forever alone.
Only seen as a rival to knock out of the way,
something to get rid of, and make way for someone else.
I am not looked upon as a friend,
I am not looked upon as a colleague, but something other.
Do I exist if I am not acknowledged?

Chantelle Lowe

Do I mean something if I am not seen as important?
I want something I do not have, I strive for it,
I try for it, but it is not there for me.
It is there for so many others, but not for me.
I strive with so many difficulties, fighting forward.

Chantelle Lowe

For the night

Where on the night,
what hold the night so young and free?
Forebode the night,
it comes a dancing, prancing through the trees.

Chantelle Lowe

For one

Give me hope where there is one,
give me time when I want some,
give me the strength I need for one.

Fragile structure

A cold and withering room,
sitting upon my own lost thoughts.
Is there where I am?
Is this where I belong?
I had thought of such,
but it is so crowded,
and I do not like it,
it frightens me.
Did I ever belong here?
To those people I see,
I wish I were not,
they are so different, yet whole.
Do I fit in,
I think not?
But it is where I am supposed to be.
I do not look frightened,
I know what this is,

Chantelle Lowe

I can sense its fragile structure.
Did I build it?
No, not I,
this was here before me,
before I ever thought.
It twists and binds me,
but I am not a part of it.
I am singled out,
like the glowing of one small flame.
But why am I singled out,
when there is so many brighter?
Because it is the turn of time,
that picks me out.
This is my time,
when others fade,
and I am left to stand.

Fragile thought

I have something said,
never let it be,
known to all the world,
what I see here,
in the time of before.
But will it come again,
and will you see it?
Is it real to your touch,
or does it comb the edges,
of your seeping smile,
does it touch your fragile eyes?
I want to see if it does,
I want to see if it opens up your thoughts,
and gains me everything I know,
or have known.
I want to bring it back,
back to me, where I am,

Chantelle Lowe

and let it die with me.

Frame of mind

Away from this world, away from any other.
Why can I not find peace?
I walk so far and this should be pleasant.
How can I control my frustration,
when they shunt me away,
as though I am nothing.
Excluding me from their little games,
yelling and screaming hateful things,
and the frustration is just so potent.
It tingles up my bones,
and changes my frame of mind.

Chantelle Lowe

Framework

Nor to hide,
nor to seek,
nor to runaway,
what is left is the framework,
with all its glory having been stripped away.

Frustration

Frustration, how does one resolve frustration,
when it is so easy to find?
Causing frustration,
how does one deal with it?
When the circumstances are against you,
when they specialise at getting what they want,
when they specialise at it everyday.
When they care only for themselves,
when no one else matters,
when hurting other people does not matter,
when hurting everyone else is something they
think they can do.

Chantelle Lowe

Get rid of this feeling

Why is this the way it has to be,
I wanted to be something,
greater than what I am.
What is it you know that I don't.
Get rid of this feeling inside my head,
make it go away.
I just want to die,
I want to get rid of this feeling.
Take it away.
I just want to be me.

Given hope

Sanity, sanity, hear my sanity.
Am I real,
or am I only a dream.
Can anybody answer me?
Is this is a dream?
The life I knew ended,
and now I have been given this one.
I don't know what to do with it.
Why was I put here?
Why was I created?
Was I meant to do something and change the world?
I feel so alone.
I am different,
yet people think I am the same.
I feel like yelling sometimes.
I was cut off from my old life,
and I do not know what to do.

Chantelle Lowe

I was reborn,
and everything I could hope for.
I was reborn,
and I could see a way out.
I was given hope,
I was granted my dreams.
This is all so much,
it is overwhelming.
I do not know what to do with it all.
It is difficult ta adjust.
I had nothing,
then I had a lot.
It is hard to cope with.
Yet it was given to me,
and I know I should do my best.

Gone

No illusion near or far,
can ever replace what I have lost.
A figure coming and going,
shall come and go no more.
Then which was once given,
is now trapped.

Grip of corrosion

Who is this person that stole me,
who cast me in nothingness.
A destroyer, a reaper of ill.
Cowering behind an opaque cover,
where society cannot see through it.
I know what the hidden thoughts are,
destroying the populace.
Laced in society's behaviour,
gleaming proud to the unseeing.
The holder of evil,
the pillar of society.
For the worst evil,
is the one that cloaks itself in good.
Taking me down, and burying me,
the tight grip of corrosion.
Eating away at my thoughts,
and self esteem.

Chantelle Lowe

In the heat of destruction,
I came forth anew.
I took hold of my own,
and away from the grip of decay.

Hard to see the light

The world slowly tears me apart and I do not know what to do.
I am so lost in something way beyond anything I understand,
and no one seems to understand me.
In all this I begin to become lost under more and more weight,
I feel it on my chest, much more than anywhere else,
it weighs me down like lead.
All this time I wonder, did I make the right decision,
when all I do is cry?
I wonder if this was meant to be, when all around me
I do not see a way out.
When all the roads are blocked and all I see is darkness,
it makes it hard to see the light.
Somewhere along the way I think I lost a little,
and all I seem to be is lost.

Chantelle Lowe

Havoc

Placement of the soul is hard to find,
in the devastating world of mine.
All the forces that combine,
play the turmoil in my mind.
All this confusion from within,
reeks havoc on my senses,
reeks havoc and tears my soul apart.

Chantelle Lowe

Heavy on the mind

Time escapes the reality of the situation,
when all is calm and quiet,
and no one calm can sense what it felt.
The turmoil from within, rising up,
from the past to weigh heavy on the mind.
This disposition besieges me as I think,
for it has made itself a part of what I am.
This was how I aimed to be,
I thought it would leave me be.
Instead I am left with this overwhelming feeling,
it is all that remains,
staying with me through every moment of my life,
to reach for me in the dark ravines.

Hiding

Time comes forth into me,
it finds and hides me.
Cover my soul and retrieves it.
Play the soul and find,
is it me you seek?
When all has gone into hiding.
Away from the real world,
steps take time, when reality has gone,
and all that is left is the hope of many.
Take my mind away from this insanity.

Hiding away

I was running, trying to keep away.
I had kept away for a very long time,
managing to hide and run to keep ahead.
Now I see them catching up,
and I am worried,
I have been running for a very long time.
I started running away from harm,
now they had changed,
I had become much older, and wearier.
When I was young I could run like the wind,
and hide with ease.
Now they were catching up,
and seeing my face all too often,
it would not take long before they knew.
I had hid among them on occasion,
when they recognised me,
I knew I would not have that option.

Chantelle Lowe

I had been caught,
and I was too close to try and leave.

Highest hope

I shall not fall down,
I seek my highest hope,
but never can reach it.

Hold on to

In the oblique and fortunate world I live in,
I hope to see and die,
for this will never be what I hold on to.

Holding myself up

It cried in my lap, I felt it in my arms,
I couldn't let it go, I knew it was a part of me.
I knew, but I couldn't reach out,
I couldn't do anything, I thought it was normal,
but it wasn't.
I wanted to let go, but I couldn't,
it ran through me, and I didn't know what to do.
I embraced it, because it was all I knew,
I embraced it because I did not know.
I wanted to die and I did not know,
no one was there to tell me, no one held out their arms,
there was no assurance that everything would be all right.
There was only me, holding myself up.
While everything died inside, and I held myself up,
and I didn't know what to do,
and all I knew, was to hold myself up.
I suffered the pain and I still feel it.

Chantelle Lowe

It comes back and I feel it.
It takes control and I feel it.
It eats me inside and I can feel it.
It kills me inside and I feel it.
I wanted someone to be there and it wasn't to be.
I wanted out and I didn't know how.
I wanted to escape and I didn't know how.
I wanted to be free and I didn't know how.
No one guided me,
my dreams were shattered and I was left there,
I couldn't understand the blindness that other people saw.
Why couldn't they see, why couldn't they see what it was doing to me.
I just wanted something so basic, I just wanted to be allowed to be me.
Even that had been denied and I could not understand.
Other people let it happen and I could not understand.
Others were ashamed to be near me and I could not understand.
All I wanted was to be me, that's all I ever wanted.

Chantelle Lowe

Holding tight

I rarely sit and play a tune,
I rarely hold and roll a dice,
I rarely call or make a sound,
I hold tight onto what I have,
I hold it in my little hand.

Chantelle Lowe

Hopeless

To see the other side,
and not turn back.
Would be hopeless,
beyond belief.

Human

I was born a female,
do you know what that means?
It means I am stricken with blood,
human blood,
it drenches my soul, and I am human.

Hurt

I was there,
that night,
it seeped into me,
and made me whole.
I laughed,
to the sky, and the stars,
for this was mine.
My freedom, and my place,
this is my home,
but not where I belong,
it is stone with no heart.
For that reason,
I have no heart,
only the ice cold touch,
of a pool so black,
and full of hurt.

Chantelle Lowe

I am not afraid

In the world I see chaos,
noise, unbearable noise.
Everything as it has been,
but it isn't,
it isn't what it was,
what it should have been.

I'm not here, I'm not here,
but I should be.
I'm standing here and I can't see,
what others do.
Help me, help me,
should I be afraid?
But I'm not,
I'm standing where I was,
where I should be,
and I am not afraid.

I cry

I cry from the bottom of my heart, I cry with all the tears in the world,
and still I do not cry enough.
I am gripped in sorrow and my tears are not enough.
I have kept my past to myself and yet that is not enough.
I cry with my blood dripping down through my hands,
and still that is not enough.
I let the blood flow freely, onto my clothes, the floor, and over the sink,
I wonder if I care anymore, when caring is too much.
Instead I just watch and wait for the flow to stop,
then I clean my clothes, and wash away the blood from the sink.
Part of me did not want me to stop, it had carried my pain away,
over the edge of the dirty surface.
I wanted it to end, and I did not know how,
all the while it could have been so nice,
but staring me in the face was a little thing called life,
and I did not want to know it.

Ignored

Ignored by the world,
treated as less than human.
Ignored and left to disaster.

Chantelle Lowe

I hold my solitude

Commotion, commemoration to expire,
within reason, I hold solitude,
which in, is held antipathy.
To exclude all successors of my wisdom,
which in turn shall do so for my opposite,
in neglect and resurrection I will always be another.
To hold on to what I have deciphered amongst others,
for the sake of my comprehensiveness,
which shall be held in my latitude of diversion.
So may conflict any who in trouble my so being,
on which forth I am brought to recommend,
the enclosure of my deficiency.
Which compounds with certainty,
my diminishing seizure,
upon my recreation, to overcome.

Chantelle Lowe

Inability to interact

Once upon a time in a garden far away,
a little girl lived.
She was small and fragile,
she knew she was different,
but she did not understand.
She knew she saw the world
from another point of view.
This child, so small and fragile,
had a very serious downfall,
not being able to communicate,
because the knowledge of how
was not to be found.
A little girl in a garden far away,
with an inability to communicate,
and socially interact.

Chantelle Lowe

In a girl's heart

In a girl's heart, I cannot decipher my ways
it is difficult to yearn my past, before.
Where I am, it will never trouble me to the deepest
moment in time.

For I have lost my virtue and goal,
yet I will not crumble, will never fail, to my own.
For somewhere, I know I will always be right
in the distance I never ponder, for here I lay to rest.
I hope I will never see my true and defiant reason
in this bleak world, I have come from.
In which my heart is constructed of every small and
docile accomplishment.

Chantelle Lowe

Incomprehensible

Detachment, hallucination, estrangement,
how can I forget what has gone before,
had I known would I have done it still?
A huge cost to my life, a huge cost on my state of mind.
A loss so great, for someone so out of place,
in a society too willing to close out people such as myself.
All my sadness burdens my soul so greatly,
it is almost incomprehensible,
all the work that was done has now come to nought.
I feel as though I have been told that the world thinks I am nothing,
and it hurts me so deeply, after everything was put forward for judgement.
Everything was put forward, and the answer was clear,
so clear that the shock was so long, and so deep.

Indifferent tide

To rise and not be seen,
up against the flood,
of an indifferent tide.

Chantelle Lowe

In dismay

Mysterious yet ponderous,
compelling with dismay.
I turn my head and look at her,
in my own special way,
and every now and then
there is,
a place I know damn well.
It comes to me,
on that sweet summer swell.
No one knows,
or no one turns a head,
To the blind little man,
on the blind little bed.
Come, come,
Say the grieving.
'Where am I?'
you said,

Chantelle Lowe

to no one in particular.
Though they all turned around,
and saw,
that piteous little painting,
on the piteous little wall.

Chantelle Lowe

In every direction

How long can it be this way,
how long can I live like this,
how long can it be?
Can it be forever?
Sometimes I am not sure,
it feeds off my soul,
slowly killing me inside.
Giving me so much grief.
It strikes me at every turn,
pulling in every direction.
How long can I remain this way?
In between places, not knowing,
is this the way I was meant to be?
Is this the journey I was meant to take,
to live like this?
How am I supposed to, when I do not know myself.
Is this what I am to ask?

Chantelle Lowe

In a world I do not understand,
I live with my own suffering
Which grasps onto what is me.
Tearing at my senses, pulling me apart,
and here I am, trying to keep myself together.

Inner strength

As all the memories filled my heart,
I saw my past and future wrapped in one.
So strong was it,
that I could see my own face,
and in my eyes I saw,
the hope that had been killed,
many years before.
It was the steady thought,
which I felt grow in my hands.
The strength of my inner soul,
which no one saw, and no one felt.
The hidden trust I held so tight,
throughout my childhood,
with all my might.
It had gone into the distance,
swept down through the flood,
of an impossible imagination.

Chantelle Lowe

In reality

Placement of time in reality.
Cosmic gift of anticipation.
Heading towards me.
At the speed of light.
The final destination,
crying, crying away.
Away to reality.

Chantelle Lowe

I run away

The shadows of darkness impel upon me,
in passions of haste I run away.
To breezes of advice I turn,
into sequels of flight I thrust.

I am the conqueror of light, yet I run from it.
I know my despair is secured.
Though I wish it not be,
so I would be able to listen
to my foe,
and suppress a reasoning.
Though I know therefore none,
and wish the same
as I know it.

Though I only know I want
so little.

Chantelle Lowe

It is too much for them,
to spare my grievance,
or focus.
As so on myself,
I wish it would only remain
for me to hold.

Internal pressure

Sliced through my precious skin,
peeled away my hope and dismay,
I knew not what lied within,
as crashing down pulled everything,
the unseen thoughts that hold and pin.

My mind is made up it screeches out,
pulls with it the tides that turn and sit,
in my eyes I close more than they can count,
writhing streams flung as the soul screamed,
tight bound it is again no pressures without.

Chantelle Lowe

Into a dream

To let go,
of something so strong,
so real,
and yet,
not there.
A time,
a place,
calling out to me.
So far away,
yet so deep.
It burrows into my thoughts,
clinging so steadily.
But the thought itself,
so fragile,
so whimsical,
so timid.
It takes time to come to the surface.

Chantelle Lowe

When it does,
it envelopes my soul,
and takes me whole.
Into a dream,
a drop of reality
echoing forth into the void.
My consciousness weeps to the ends of my mind.
There is nothing which can tell me not.
For this is so,
and I cannot change,
the deepest reason of a cause unheard of.

Chantelle Lowe

Into nothing

One time and I could not imagine,
that my impact could mean so little.
It washed away into nothing,
in the presence of those who held influence.
And in that way blocks me,
and crucifies my stance.
For I have nothing left to give,
more than what I have given.
I gave all I could,
and for that I received nothing.
I showed them my soul and who I was,
and it was torn up and thrown out,
and left me with nothing of myself.

Inspiration

Inspiration,
calls away,
like a feeling,
in disarray.
With the day,
to rise again,
with no idea,
what will happen then.
No place,
to call away the sin,
of other places,
and so begin.
With no design,
within the mind,
to work away,
and come to find.
A place alone,

Chantelle Lowe

and in relation,
to those around,
yet its own creation.

Chantelle Lowe

In time

Nothing is as it was,
trespassing on time.
Raging forward in time.

Invisible

A child small and humble,
glimpsing out at the world.
A child's small hand reaching,
slapped back.
A small child ignored, overlooked,
invisible in the world outside.
A small child reaching out,
and no one hears.
A tiny silhouette in the background,
a small meek voice inaudible.
Ignored and left by the world,
ignored and left behind.
The small child learns to be lonely,
is not to be hit or shouted at.
The small child hides,
but the one that sees it is not the
one that cares for it.

Chantelle Lowe

The child hides, but it cannot hide
enough to escape.
A child taken away by the only person
in the world who cares.
Its mother.

Chantelle Lowe

Irreplaceable

Time is irreplaceable to the soul.
Can I see beyond the day,
when I cannot see beyond me.

Chantelle Lowe

It has meaning

A poem isn't something that can be,
chosen by one particular type of person,
and be expected to be liked by another.

A poem is only liked by someone,
if they can relate to it,
the better they can relate to it,
and appreciate it.

A poem is very personalised way,
of writing,
if the individual can not relate to it,
its meaning is overlooked.

I will remain

As I see the dying hand,
crumble into dismay.
I wonder now, where I stand,
with sorrow leading the way.

No hand can I hold for comfort,
in a place where I must hold my own,
and every step moves with effort,
where shallow waters lie and groan.

I see the way, deceitful,
glimmering as though in harmony.
When I know this place to be hurtful,
beyond all expectancy.

I know the path is long and hard,
with all the building pain.

Chantelle Lowe

Even though the truth is marred,
I know I will remain.

Judgement

A world where how good you are is judged by other people.
How well you do is judged by other people.
You have no say in that.
It is other people who are around you.
Your feelings and nature are based around that judgement.
Your career and future are based around that judgement.
All our lives we work to please the opinions
that other people have concerning us.
Is it worth the trouble, the life long battle?
Sometimes it is hard to say.
For most people it is too much, stress falls upon them.
Once they stood so tall but now it is too much.
We should not expect a lot from people, it is very easy to fall under stress.
People may joke but we are all sensitive, in our own individual ways.
That can't be helped, we are all like that to one another, in our own ways,
even though we may not realise it.

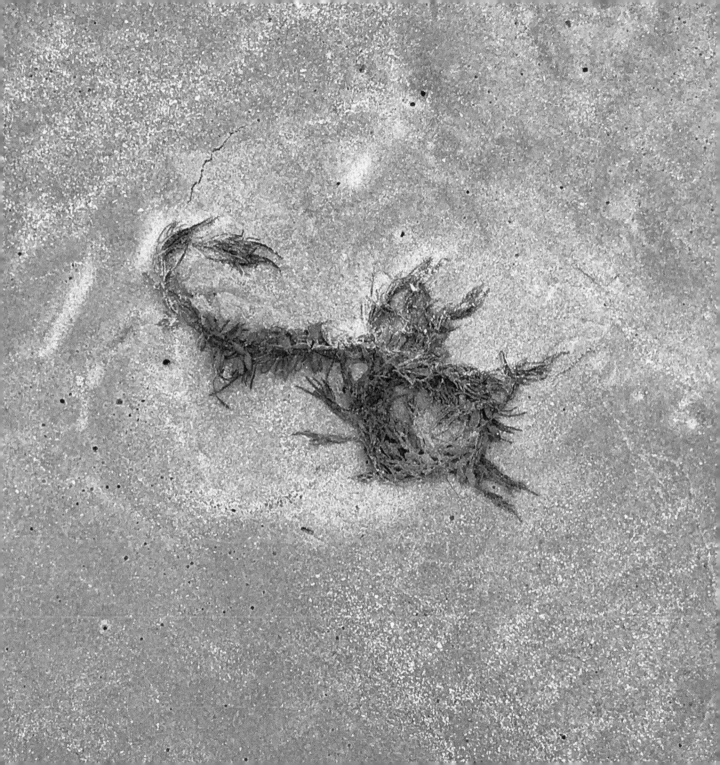

Chantelle Lowe

Left alone

It hurts,
but I can't express it.
It's like a feeling,
that comes and goes,
and never looks back,
always looks back,
on me,
in me,
around me,
everywhere.
I can feel it,
in my mind,
it is trapped,
in me.
I can't get it out,
it won't go away.
It wont let me know what it is,

Chantelle Lowe

won't let me grasp it,
hold it,
or touch it,
reach it.
I can only feel it,
sense it.
It won't leave me alone,
I want to go away,
get away from it.
Please don't hurt me,
please don't leave me.
I want you to stay,
I want everything to stay.
I want to be alone,
to be left alone,
in peace,
no emotion,
no infliction,
no scar,
to feel,
as I do in me.

Let me be myself

In the undaunted awakening,
let myself be myself to myself,
to resume the peace of disputing,
to the acknowledgement of my stealth.

Welcome hither my friend to my side,
for with none I will have peace in me,
a tranquil refuge not to abide,
for leads a trail of insanity.

I observe many, though I know few,
for them, I am not more than a shadow,
to me I am great, not so to you,
I stay with me always, and you? No.

Which to me, I understand myself,
that I hold, my sentimental wealth.

Chantelle Lowe

Letting go

Rumbling through rummages and time long forgotten,
here I sit and stand.
Over and over I see the waves,
lapping over and through my precious skin,
but I haven't come here for that, I have come to test myself,
my strength, my virtue.
All held forward on a brilliant ray,
parading itself towards the presumptuous sphere,
which I lay deep within my hands, waiting for the oncoming conclusion.
That which I want to shed,
place a hold on,
then blissfully watch it promoting from without.
I did have hold of it, I swear I did,
but I had to let go,
let it run through the bareness
of my fingers and drench into the emanating flow.

Chantelle Lowe

Life

Carry on to be,
what though I see,
not shall I find,
though it to me bind.
Nor too far shall I go,
for here I am so.
Neither shall I accomplish,
for I have already come to abolish,
that so I find missing,
the most wonted and valuable thing.

Chantelle Lowe

Lifting my head

I suppose that if I lift my head, I can find what I want,
but what if I don't,
what if nothing will change?
Something must, but what?
I don't know, I don't ever know,
but for me that doesn't really matter.

Little voice

Inside there is a little voice
wanting to get out,
inside that voice is me.

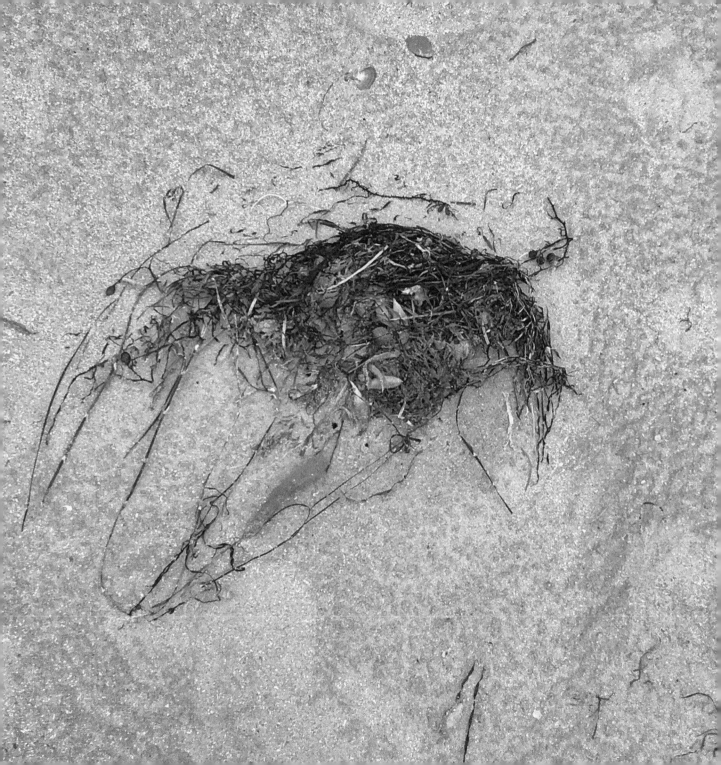

Loneliness

What it's like to be lonely,
in a world full of hidden truth.
Many doors that stay closed to you,
when they lay wide open for many others.
To feel as though everyone who speaks to you hides something you should
know,
but only shatters you with lies.
And you can't understand why they are doing this,
why they are treating you as though you aren't there or don't exist.
Or they think you are not worthy of them.
Or they are using you, misguiding you towards something you don't want.
You feel rejected by people you thought were friends,
the only ones you can rely on are betraying you.
All the time you try and look for a way out,
but you are nowhere near your dreamed of goal.
Your only hope, that can ever shed its true and warming light on you,
one that you imagine in your head.

Chantelle Lowe

But in your real world there is only false light, false hope,
that will always look dark and down upon you.
Expect you will try, as all you might to shake it off,
it will always smother your failing hope,
which you will never be able to reach.

Lonely inside

Faithful are the dead,
lonely are the living.
I have found someone,
yet I am still lonely inside,
it is a loneliness which cannot easily be fixed.
Here I am left to deal with it.
It takes me in,
and feeds off me.

Lost dreams

My sorrow is immense, it seeps through my heart,
like the tempered rain that washes away the windows,
of our souls.
It finds me,
oh why does it find me?
Am I the only one to have it in the gap of
my lost heart?
Why can't it leave me, why cannot I find rest?
That would be cheerful, oh so cheerful,
to drape off my ragged sorrows,
of a lost and lonely cry, which tares through me,
as the shattered shards of thousands of pieces,
of gleaming metal,
tear at my soul and numb my pain.
My heartless, agonising cries,
screaming through my body.
It didn't work!

Chantelle Lowe

But it didn't work, it didn't help,
all my efforts blown away to nothing, and what for?
My own dream.
That didn't work, it failed, I lost my hope,
my happiness and everything with it.
Why did I kill those dreams?
Those beautiful dreams.

Lost within

Lost it,
I didn't have it to begin with,
It did not exist within me.
It is not something that I can fathom.

Manifesting

Anonymity in diversion, can lead to complication.
This is supposed to be what is, even in isolation.
Hearing, calling, to what is, being loved and knowing what is.
Anticipation ranging from high to low,
and in all of this imagination spreading through all.
This deliberate attempt crowning expectation,
striving to achieve in the attempt.
Placing gratitude and thankfulness side by side.
Manifesting the ideas of the self.

Manipulate

In the ebony room,
I see a ray of light,
it streams down on me.
I take it and transform it,
into my own manipulation,
it ceases to exist as it so did.
I have changed it into something else,
a form as unique as my own,
yet very different in a compelling way.
I know not what to think or do,
in my transparent world of virtue.

Chantelle Lowe

Maze of deception

The instant that felt,
tremors lifting up from the ground.
Not knowing where to run in all this.
In a maze of deception,
somewhere lies the truth,
seeping up through the hairline fractures,
to cover the immense surface,
covered with so much pain.
The turmoil creeps through my existence,
it extends out through the course of my body.
I have no idea what it is,
yet somehow it was predetermined.
Picking me out,
taking me as I am.
Not planning anything,
existing in the moment.

Mend the soul

Trial of trust taken away,
innocence taken away.
An attempt to pick up the left over pieces,
after the disfigurement and mutilation of a soul.
How is it possible to trust again,
when there is so much building to be done.
The soul was left incomplete with gaping holes,
needing tentative repairs amidst the gloom.
Is it possible to mend such devastating damage?
Is it possible to heal the good left in the soul?
The power to move on has to be great to overcome,
and conquer the torture of the past.
Still riding against the manipulation of cruelty,
it walks the long fight ahead, away from dispassion.
A glimmer of the identity begins to form against the harm,
a long time coming from underneath the veil of deceit.
It is fragile in its new form,

Chantelle Lowe

an elegant silhouette.

Chantelle Lowe

Mistaken

And the world with all its ashes came tumbling down.
it deranged the places of the mind, and came out to play.
Coming forth from unseen places, taking a turn into density.
What has gone, was gone before, it held no ground.
Sweeping across the faces, mimicking the time wasted,
and for all eternity, it was real, creeping up into life.
Taking hold, not knowing where, not knowing how.
It was the creepiest, darkest sensation taking hold.
No thinking of ever after in the grip of insanity.
I placed my mind, and I knew it not.
What were these thoughts, these sensation?
Criss-crossing what could have been mistaken for normality.
Interrupting hideous thoughts telling me to like it,
and take pleasure from what harmed, warping reality.
When this is what it was, what it always had been.

Chantelle Lowe

My curse

Please help me to destroy,
for I do not have it in me.
Instead I falter,
and run on mindless anger,
covered in the envelope of sadness.
Sadness so extreme,
it fills me in a way I know not how.
It is there and I cannot be rid of it.
I feel it in my soul,
it pains me in a way I cannot understand.
This I have to live with,
this which is my curse.

Chantelle Lowe

My path

In the dark blue yonder,
I see a shimmering light,
their light, their hope,
their dreams.
I am there,
I am walking amongst them,
skimming past unnoticed.
Yet when they turn,
they touch, they burn.
They sear through me,
heedless of what I do,
I do not know them,
and I do not want them.
Yet their imprints are there,
on my self conscious,
and when I wake I find,
that I am still there,

Chantelle Lowe

that it was no dream.
I use all the strength I have,
to hold them high over my head,
and away from my thought,
my symbolic hope,
so that my path is free,
for me to tread on,
and no one, but no one,
shall stand in my way.

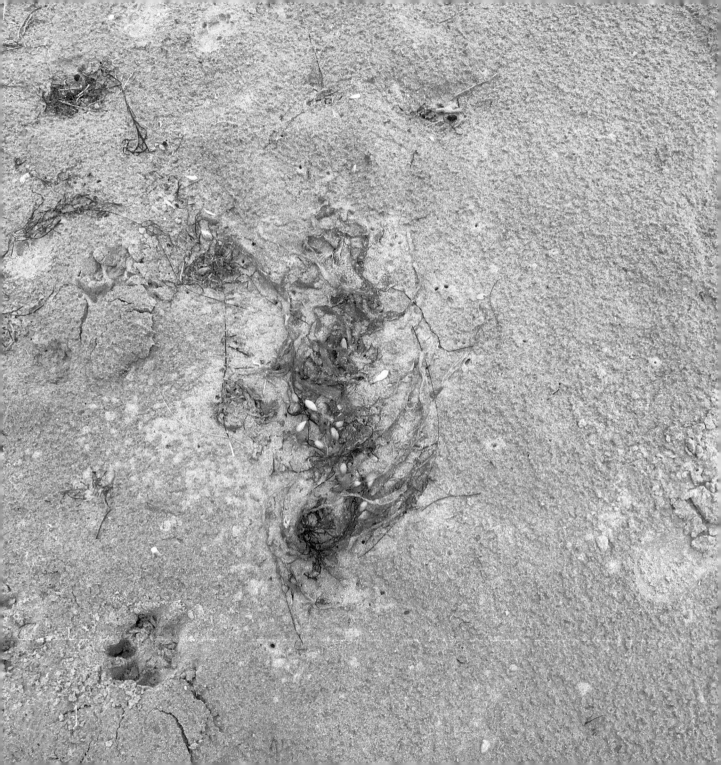

Chantelle Lowe

Myself

I am myself,
I am no other,
I'm not an actress.

Chantelle Lowe

My thought flows

In the coming of time,
I see upon myself,
the rhythm of others,
in which my ideology flows.
To gather in the basis,
of my possessing thoughts,
in the dreams of my satisfaction,
and consciousness.

Chantelle Lowe

Needed to know

There is no right, there is no wrong,
there is only me, and how I feel.
This is all that matters now,
this is all I have ever needed to know.

Chantelle Lowe

No longer needed

Flowing am I, into the desolation,
of another's creation,
made against me.
Another's creation, I turn away,
for my own to see.
A glimmer of hope,
a realisation, that this was not meant to be,
once friends, suddenly parted,
out of convenience no longer needed.
Am I expected to feel grateful,
for something that didn't really exist.

Chantelle Lowe

No one hears

To ponder upon the wind of time,
seeing what is left.
When no one hears,
the echoing calls,
raging through my head.

No one helped

Who?
Who will care for the children,
when they are gone?
Who will care for their nameless souls,
when their suffering has ended,
because no one helped?

Chantelle Lowe

No one speaks

If I were walking in the wood,
what would I see, what would I do?
I have come to no conclusion,
but if you knew would you dare say?
Would you dare say at all?
But you don't and you won't, and that is what intrigues me,
but no one comes.
No one dares say, dares say a word, at all,
but what would you say?
If you knew at all, all the things that were,
what would you say?
I wonder so all night and day, but does it matter,
to anyone? I guess not,
and I guess that you would some day know, anyway.

No other

I cannot see my way ahead,
the beginning has no end.
Where I see one day rise,
I see no other.

Chantelle Lowe

No patience

I hear destiny calling me.
It is a patience
I seem to call
as a feeling
towards it.
It reaches out to me,
I have no patience.
All I see
is today,
not tomorrow,
nor the future.

No possible way

In a deep and darkened house,
in the middle of one corner,
there lies an old oak tree.
If you put your hand up against it,
you can feel its living soul,
moving ever so slowly,
up.
Towards warmth and freedom,
and the harshness of the elements,
they soar, the branches of its feelings,
so high and so close,
coming down upon one another,
then back again.
I hear them calling out to me,
through the years and the pain and the agony,
it seeps through the harshest sounds,
and conquers everything I know,

Chantelle Lowe

but I can't go back,
I mustn't.
It will destroy everything,
though I can feel the pull of its force,
so strong against my limbs.
So harsh the impact,
but there is no possible way,
it can take me,
that I know so sorely,
and so painfully.

Chantelle Lowe

Not for me

I could hear the children playing in the distance,
laughing.
I disliked their laughter,
it was not for me.

No time

No time,
no chance
lay upon my mind.

Chantelle Lowe

Not my home

I stand here alone,
this is not my place,
this is not my home.

Chantelle Lowe

Not near me

Where I sit the shadows grow,
the light out the window seems,
to shine in one place, not near me.

Chantelle Lowe

Not so sure

Why am I the one,
that it calls to with seduction.
It wants me, it wants my very soul,
reaching out to the edges,
seeping forward.
It cries alone, inside of me.
It wants to know who I am,
but what can I say,
when I do not know the answer.
Did I really ever know?
Because now I'm not so sure.

Not to bother

To deliver from whence they came,
from afar to play the game.
I did not know it at the time,
I did not see the paradigm.
Just glimpsing around the corner,
like something small, not to bother.

Chantelle Lowe

Not yours

I hear your voice,
I am the power in your hand.
I hear your words,
but I am not yours.

Chantelle Lowe

Not yours to claim

How dare you come in and destroy what I have,
it is not yours to trample on.
You who has no intelligence and holds only disrespect for others.
When others treat you as you treat them,
you react in total stupidity showing it for all to see,
what you really are.
Your features and clumsiness warns other people of what you are.
You who think you have the right to molester and abuse others,
and have them treat you as king.
You wonder why this does not happen,
and you scream and throw things when they treat you
how you treat them.
You ugly ogre of dirt and pain, you are not worthy of respect.
You deserve your punishment twice and worse,
to show you what it is like,
how you make other people feel about you.
You who deserves worse than nothing,

Chantelle Lowe

when you die I will dance with joy,
and while you are still alive I will spit on your face,
and that will still be less than your right to claim.

Chantelle Lowe

No warmth

In a room I sit, with lights,
and nothing else.
No love, no comfort,
no warmth.

Chantelle Lowe

No way out

I wish it were just the usual things, but it's not.
They're real, so real
and I can name them,
but can't say a word, one single word.
I've been trapped for so long
and shown no way out.

Old owl

In the Canterbury tree lives an old owl,
whose eyes are big as bronze plates,
and wings stretch as far as the tree is tall.
It's an old tree, as old as the owl who lives there,
in the night you can hear him calling.

When the moon's light reaches the far,
side of the river I am free to find,
my eternal power and use it with all my wisdom.
I shall search every place to make sure,
there is no harm tonight.
When the moon's light reaches the near side,
of the river I return tired without,
A soul of energy, my power ceased.
Then I shall rest again to avoid the light,
of day which with it brings the prying,
eyes of others.

Chantelle Lowe

This owl is my keeper, my keeper of wisdom,
each night he comes to me just before he returns.
He comes to my place tattered and wounded,
I heal him, while he is there we chat.

Chantelle Lowe

One of them

If I wish I can be there,
as well as you,
in the support of many,
against those who hold back,
in fear of themselves,
who dispossessed,
their own,
to protect falseness,
in itself.
Theirs,
in contribution,
they huddle,
to selfishness,
why me I ask,
why one of them.

Chantelle Lowe

One so dark

Here is me and what I am.
Discovering the complexity of memories,
which resides itself in me.
This complexity shapes who I am.
It begins with a very dark picture,
so dark it covers all that is hope.
It shapes my world,
and it shapes what is.
This is the world that created me.
One so dark I barely knew what I was.
It moulded me in many ways,
creating the edges of despair which covers me now,
it made me from this dark picture,
it created my living soul.
It darkened the world I live in,
as it darkens all my dreams.
It is killing me now,

Chantelle Lowe

as I see it again and again.

One step away

Nobody can tell who I am.
I am a person,
with a single mind,
and a single body.
I have a way,
which leads a path,
to follow,
and to exist.
I do not see my fate,
but I know I have found reason.
One step away,
is ultimate freedom.
A paradise inferno,
in which all becomes everything,
And nothing is one.
How else does one find,
the way to lead,

and guide itself forward,
into existence?
Nothing else can matter,
where no one has found
what is right,
and all is hope
in denial.
Where one can reach,
what is.
When what is,
is all I see.
In a place where hell is born,
and purity takes over.
I am there,
in between.
Neither one nor the other,
yet both,
all at once,
reaching forward,
as I slice my way.
The ravine calls me down,
to where I am,
and I can see no human touch,
where my hand has lain.

Chantelle Lowe

For I am not as I was,
nor will I ever be,
in a place so hard to find.
It calls with no uncertainty,
to where I am.

Chantelle Lowe

On the edge

As far as the eye could see,
and further.
I stood on a ledge,
so high above the whim of the mortal world.
My foot stood part way over the edge,
as I looked down.
I could hear the sounds behind me,
but not below.
All was small and fragile,
from the bird's eye,
all quarrels held only a minor significance,
and were extinguished in the time,
of a single flame.
I stood with the breath taking view,
one jump, and I could have been part of it,
but that was not what I did.

Chantelle Lowe

Open to nothing

Why is it,
that I have nothing,
when I open my hands?

Chantelle Lowe

Overwhelming

Hence forth into the night I go, never looking back,
yet in all my ways it appears to be broken,
not seeing, not believing, just being straight.
How far do I go when I do not see,
all that you have put in front of me?
Killing pain, killing sanity.
Overwhelming the already burdened soul.

Part of me

I wanted to let go,
to get out of the picture I was in.
When it had crushed me so harshly,
it had come down and damaged all my hopes.
How can something be so cruel?
How can something like that hurt so much?
How can it not care what it does?
It had hurt me so badly and not cared,
it had left me on my own to heal,
and my wound was so deep,
that I left part of me behind.
I had trapped it away from the world,
so that it could not be hurt.

Chantelle Lowe

Passed me by

Nothing is as it was,
when all came to an end.
I did not know who I was,
to have done such a thing.
When all I had done,
was far from it.
To be called the opposite,
to who I was,
when I had achieved so little,
but knowing nothing else.
Whatever was wrought by hatred,
had been withered from sight, away.
No one fought, what no one heard,
even though I tell a lie.
All in hatred was not lost,
when I knew what passed me by.

Chantelle Lowe

Patience

I wait,
what do I wait for?
For you to realise,
but when will that happen?
Never.

Chantelle Lowe

Patiently

In the ebony room I sit,
waiting patiently,
here the wind blows all day,
never calming down.

Chantelle Lowe

People that go by

What comfort does university give?
When I have no friends to find me there.
My class is full of people that go by,
I try to stop and chat a while.
But then they leave me behind.
When I wanted to go to university,
I did not think it would be this lonely.
I knew I was making sacrifices,
but I thought I would meet friends.
I go to my classes,
and I know no one.
I could be a shadow,
and they would not notice.
I am put down regularly,
by students and teachers alike.
I am not sure if they mean to,
but when I leave,

Chantelle Lowe

I have no family with me,
I open my front door,
and I am alone.

Prerequisite

Here it could be said that I am left undecided,
I know not how to react to the new invasion or lack of it.
Claiming space without person, living without being.
It is a strange prerequisite
but how am I to know any other.

Chantelle Lowe

Prison of time

You know your troubles cease,
when others begin.
Here in the world where all is lost,
or so I have been told,
and the way life outside,
is oh so cold.
But in my prison of time,
I begin to wonder,
is it really me
that I am afraid of?

Time does not make sense,
when others have left,
to find further places.
In this world away from what was,
in the hour which creates what is.
Playing time through its fingers,

Chantelle Lowe

making sounds away from comfort,
and fleeting by with treachery.
Taking up the mask,
as it empties over the hand that holds it.

Proclamation

My diversion is but a small one, in which I belong to,
though I only feel as if I have never been there.
In my home coming I consider myself, my own,
yet in time I will find out whether or not
my proclamation, is in my belief.

Quietly

Quietly, quietly, oh so quietly,
so that no one may know
that I am having difficulty.
For sometimes it is easier
if I pretend that
everything is all right.
Quietly, quietly, oh so quietly,
so that no one will hear
that I am having problems.
For I am used to
having no one
who understands.
Quietly, quietly, oh so quietly,
so that no one will see
me suffering.
For people usually
misinterpret that

Chantelle Lowe

for being lazy.
Quietly, quietly, oh so quietly,
because almost nobody understands.

Reaching forward

The child holds out her hand and reaches forward.
No one hears, no one knows, because no one cares.
The child holds out her hand,
and the imaginary world meets it,
because the real world will not.
In this imaginary world the people listen,
the people take the child away from the harm.
They protect this child,
when no one in the real world will.
They give her a home,
a place to believe in,
something to hold onto.
They comfort the child,
when everyone else walks away.
An imaginary world that gives more than the real one.
People who care more than those who are real.
This child spends more time in the imaginary world than the real.

Reach out my hand

I cannot get rid of that which I see,
it possess me and influences me.
A transient time for a transient space,
it culminates inside of me.
I wanted it, I wanted what it had to offer,
yet I am unable to use it.
No one's help brought me here,
yet I reach out my hand.
No realism exists to my dream,
it is a fantasy, a world where my skills are valued,
a world where I have skills.
I can be me, and I am accepted for who I am.
This reality which overcomes me is not the
reality which I seek, it is no the reality
which I desire.
I want to be known,
to have friends, real friends,

Chantelle Lowe

but I do not have them.
Where are they when I am all alone,
they turn away, not wanting to know,
not wanting to have anything to do with me.
They do not see me as a friend.
In that way I am alone.
I am alone,
I have only myself to comfort.
I am crying on the inside,
and I do not know what to do.

Reappear

Waves, waves, caressing my soul,
trying to hurt me, and break me apart.
Letting me be, but not as it were,
with all my thoughts and memories.
Trapped inside my head,
waiting to reappear.
In a time I do not see,
my final destruction,
but here is nothing of use to me,
in this moment of revelation.

Chantelle Lowe

Relief

I troubled myself as I sat,
the pain was still there in my side,
and I wanted relief.
In a strange sort of way it had given me that.
A short relief from this world,
that keeps trying to take me under.
In a way it brought me closer to myself,
closer to who I had been,
I found myself admitting things had gone wrong,
and I cried in a pool of deprivation.
Was I looking for myself?
I was not sure of that either.
In some way I had more of a past
than most people.
From the moment of my birth on,
I had a great deal to find out,
and some I already knew.

Chantelle Lowe

Run from fate

As I see the world,
I die from it,
hoping I will live again.
This is not for me,
this lonely land,
I have held too long my peace.
Such is fate,
yet I run from it.

Chantelle Lowe

Safe place

I want to go home,
to a place where I am always happy,
that will be my home.
A place I can imagine,
and be safe.

Same situation

I find myself unable to cope again,
stuck in the same situation.
I do not know exactly how to get out,
I wish there were some other way.
I try to break out of the mess I am in,
yet it gets harder every day.
I want to deal with things better than this,
I want to be able to try.
Yet my best efforts seem to come undone,
when I head towards my fear.
My life has only just begun,
and I wipe it away in fear.

Chantelle Lowe

Say my piece

I want to get away from their awful stares,
I want to scream and shout.
I want to break free,
keep my individuality.
I want to stay in one piece,
and crush them under one foot.
I want to stop their little rumours,
and stand up for myself.
I want to be an individual,
not hauled down by all their garbage.
I long for the day I can be myself,
I would be so proud.
It would be so nice to stare down at them,
and make them feel inadequate,
make them feel small and insignificant.
I want to soar,
I want to glide with every step,

Chantelle Lowe

speak my mind,
and say my piece,
be strong and pass them by.
I want to be the person inside of me.

Scar

I look up,
and see blood on the concrete.
I see my father working in the garden,
I see him drop the tool,
and come running.
He is scared,
he is by my side,
and looking at me.

I see my mother,
she is pressing a wet flannel to my forehead,
I am sitting down,
my father is gone.

I can see my mother sitting in the front seat of the car,
I am sitting in the back,
I am pressing the flannel to my forehead.

Chantelle Lowe

I take a quick look at the flannel,
I am curious,
It is filled with blood,
dark, nearly black.
My mother is starting the engine of the car.

I am lying on a hospital bed,
there are hospital beds to either side of me,
they are empty.
My mother is beside me,
we are in a large room,
we are alone,
and waiting.

I see people in green,
they put a sheet over me,
it is green.
There is a hole in it,
not for my eyes,
all I see is green.
I can feel them hurting me,
where I am bleeding.
I am struggling,
I pull the sheet off,

Chantelle Lowe

everything is green,
the room.
There are lights,
my mother is there,
so are the people,
wearing green.
They shove the green sheet back over my eyes,
they start hurting me again,
I am struggling.

I see a man,
he is wearing green,
he is putting stickers on my cut,
he says they are butterfly stickers.
I am sitting on the table where they hurt me,
he holds a mirror in front of me,
so that I can see what they did,
I get off the table.

I look in the mirror,
and I see my right eyebrow,
it is perfect.
I see my left,
there is a scar,

Chantelle Lowe

it cuts into my eyebrow,
on the outer corner,
parallel to the top of my eye.
When I think about my scar,
I see myself again lying on the operating table,
the surgeon starts to sew my cut.
I hurl the green sheet off my covered eyes,
and I see the bright lights in the green room,
with the green surgeons, and my mother.
I was four,
I feel helpless,
scared,
alone,
and hurt.
I did a sketch of my face,
my left eyebrow has a dent in it.
That is my memory,
that is my scar.

Searching

To do too much,
to do too little.
'What is the right way', we say. What is the wrong way?
Or how can you tell at all.
Is one person's imagination as good as another, or better.
Who knows, who can say. I won't, I won't dare say.
I won't dare speak the final word.
'It isn't here!' they say, 'It isn't here!' Screaming in agony.
'Where could it have gone! Who has it?'
No one knows, and no one will say.
'It isn't up to me' I say, for that wasn't the way at all.
I knew, I never told them, I never meant to.
It was here. It was here all along,
but no one could find it,
because it wasn't,
what they
were looking for.

Secret child

Secret child of the night, where do you run?
Do you run away from me,
when I could be there for you?
I know your life was harsh,
I saw it, I lived it.
I was there with you, when all those things happened.
I know you wanted to cry out,
reach out and find those who cared.
It burdened my soul to know you,
and know what you were going through.
It was not easy, though I knew it was the way.
Creation made, time lost,
pain dealt with alone.
I come here for you, and I know you,
because you were my past.
You did not live in vane,
you lived for me, and I am grateful.

Chantelle Lowe

Sense of being

I sleep, not knowing what is behind me,
nor what may lay in front.
For time is an energy without a reason,
losing the sense of being.

Chantelle Lowe

Sharpness

As I crossed the road,
on my palm the sharpness felt,
it was warm with the heat,
did neither cut my hand nor,
help heal what had been, and lost.

Small request

Process of the mind,
it takes, it gives.
Collaboration.
I wanted something so simple,
yet my past denied it to me.
It seemed so easy for the others,
but so difficult for me.
I wanted to know,
I wanted to belong,
but it was kept from me.
A small and simple request,
and I was shunned out of the way.
Kept to the side,
and taken for granted,
lied about and silenced away.

Chantelle Lowe

So close

In the outside of the house,
two people come.
'Who are they?' I said,
but no one hears.
I cry out in pain, but no one is there to help.
It is cold, but I hear them,
closer now, closer than before.
It is dark and damp, I am searching for them,
they are there, I can feel them,
calling out to me.
They are a long way off,
I feel them closer,
they are close, so close.

So deep

I have an overwhelming sadness,
so deep inside me,
it is hard to keep.

Chantelle Lowe

Solace

Everything is not as it was,
as it was supposed to be.
In this world of dismay and solace.

Chantelle Lowe

Spirit

I am one,
I will not let me be taken,
shall not be my soul destroyed,
shall never my dreams be disturbed.
For I will live on inside of me,
and no one can take that away,
from me.

Still nothing

Carrying through on promises perceived by individuals,
a lesson unlearned, yet remedied.
Touching the tip of the iceberg,
not wanting to look back.
I reach out, I have nothing,
I give so much, I try my hardest,
yet I receive nothing.
I try beyond my hardest,
yet still nothing.
As a young girl I had the confidence,
which was quickly beaten out of me.
Instead I have been installed with someone else's program,
and I cannot get rid of it.

Chantelle Lowe

Suffer the same

In the hollow of darkness, everything stayed white,
for I knew not what I saw,
when everything came undone at my lap.
Did you know which way you went,
when I could not see you anymore.
Did I call out and find you sitting there,
in the oblivion of nothingness.
I liked you more as a figment of my imagination,
when you could not hurt me the way you did.
I see you still there in my mind's eye,
when all the luck drains away from my day.
I wanted to get to know you properly,
in some ways I already know you too well.
Did it have to be that way,
everything that has since past.
I know not, when I hope that no one suffers the same,
as I have at your hand.

Suggestions

These are only suggestions,
I suppose that you do not look at them,
instead look through them and past them.

Chantelle Lowe

Sure of

In a wondrous world what am I living for?
These daily tasks which predetermine my existence,
and yet I do not see what is ahead.
Is it for me, I am not sure.
But what I am sure of is me.

Tainted minds

The trial I am on is great,
the cost is plenty.
I cannot see how,
or why they could treat me that way.
It is so easy for them,
with their groups and their friends.
They turn their eyes away in scorn,
their seething words sprawl from their tongue.
They chastise and lie,
and keep me out.
They keep me away from their groups,
and taunt me with their silence.
It is a growing suffering of unhealthy attitudes,
seeping from the corners of their souls,
and into their tainted minds.

Chantelle Lowe

Talent

Aspire to assist, creating inequity,
in disillusionment.
Creating the need for aspiration.
Talent is an unreasoned soul,
writhing and wriggling,
waiting to get out.
To be let out and take control.

Take away calm

Taking away calm in the precipice of day.
I might have said it was worse,
but then I was not so sure,
and with a blink of an eye,
all was gone from my hand.
I stood, self conscious,
and a part of me felt relieved.
It was the way of the world,
and I was not.

Chantelle Lowe

Taken are my dreams

Who kills my dreams at night,
who takes them all away?
With a fist,
then crushes them.
I loved so dearly,
all of them.

The coldest day

Covering under blankets long forgotten,
having travelled a lifetime away.
The smallest comfort having meaning,
on the cold and darkest day.
It saw me through my lonely years,
when others were out having fun.
On the night when I would study late,
it would be a cosy place for one.
Something to meet the smallest needs,
when starving to pay the rent.
It comforted me through saddened times,
when little assistance was sent.
Like a worn out friend it saw me through,
the darkest hours I ever had.
While everything came crashing down,
it saw me when I was sad.
A little cloud of happiness,

Chantelle Lowe

amidst the outside mess.

Chantelle Lowe

The only person

When I was young, I could see the children play,
all around, I used to watch them,
I could feel their joy and hurt.
I used to dream, by myself because that was,
the only person I had.
I used to walk,
backwards and forwards, because I had no friends,
no one to lean on, no one to have fun with.
The only time anyone took any notice of me,
was not to be my friend.

Chantelle Lowe

The quiet

In the dead of night,
I saw the light,
all shimmering and grey.
It was so calm,
it was so quiet,
I thought it was all gone,
but when I crept,
upon my toes,
the splendour was a sight.
But in the end,
I mocked them all,
and so was left quiet.

Chantelle Lowe

The way I cry

I am coming into awareness.
I do not yet know
why.
I see a different ending,
and a different way.
Time does not see me,
or the way I cry.

Through desolation

Disappointment leads to a road of sadness,
I know I can not cope,
but I must go forward.
Onward through the desolation,
through the despair and betrayal.
It comes together to envelope the drops,
of tears down my cheek.
I cover up the hurt from being excluded,
I try my best to carry on.
It goes beyond simple recognition,
to something far more sinister.
It is likely that I will walk away,
with no friends to be found.

Chantelle Lowe

Through the open window

In the dull room, I see a ray of light,
winding itself far,
down the walls and onto the worn, colourful carpet.
Which with its brightness dissolved the warmth,
spreading it through out the small room.
I looked up to the ceiling and the sky above,
through my open windows.
My mind soared into the clouds,
and I was free.

Time of attitudes

A time of attitudes,
a time of reconciliation.
I wish it was that,
but it is not.
I sometimes wish I could pretend a lie,
but I already know,
truth is hard as ice.

Chantelle Lowe

Time makes no sense

My life is a mixture of ups and downs,
where eternity takes an hour,
and time itself makes no sense,
I hear the call coming from afar,
and I do not realise what it is.
I tracked my life to this point in time,
and I am not so sure of what I have done.
I took away my own hope for another,
and it seems a difficult choice.
Then, I am not sure if I ever wanted.

Chantelle Lowe

To be

To be,
to be none,
to be one.
I alone, and I alone shall see.

Chantelle Lowe

To be complete

It is in here somewhere, where is it?
I can't find it, I've lost it somewhere in the depths of grey.
It is hiding, I can see it, no I've lost it,
but I shall find it another day.
When it is calm, and I can hear the wind whistling,
through the panes of glass, and the substance taking form,
but not in the way they see.

It comes, calling, calling through the many seas, but it is waiting,
hiding and waiting, for just that one person to come along,
then it shall be complete.

To be trapped

Trapped,
in a world of non-understanding.
Obliterated,
in a piece of time,
unable to make a move.
Come,
I wish I did not fear.
See,
I am what I will always be.
Here,
lies my question still unknown.
To wake,
and not be challenged,
is a trap.

Too close

Why cannot people leave me be,
they come too close,
so many, all around me.
I try to move, break free,
but they are everywhere.
I cannot get rid of their feeling.
They smother me,
I hate and detest them.
They create things so horrible,
beyond redemption.
Taking their place, and tainting others.
Coming forward out of the light,
and creating insanity.
Corrupting thoughts and ideas,
destroying everything which surrounds me.
Ripping at my soul.
I will not let them destroy

Chantelle Lowe

who I am.

Chantelle Lowe

Topple over

Pull at my senses,
and topple me over,
am I the one to lose?
Call me through time,
and change my way,
did I not see you there?
I am only one,
all by myself,
I cannot find who I am.

To reach out

The flow of golden ebony running like a tide,
seeps through my numb fingers into the source below.
It creates an antagonism, do I remember?
Do I forget?
Where do I place blame, when so many are at fault?
They just accepted this and offered no help,
they gave no support when it was so obvious.
Sometimes I asked why, why did others let it continue,
when it could have been so easy to reach out a hand.
In part I feel alone, because people saw and turned away,
it was all right for them, but it was I who could not leave.
When everybody went I was left there, I still do not understand.
I wanted so badly to leave, yet I was so young.
I wanted to be brave and run away, but I could not.
I was trapped in a world I did not want to be in,
I was trapped in someone else's insanity.
When everyone else ran, because they could,

Chantelle Lowe

when everyone else played ignorant, because they could,
when it was me who was dealt the blow.

Chantelle Lowe

Torn between two worlds

In the dismal hall of failure,
I look around.
It deludes me, this substance,
of fine texture.
I created it,
but it is not within me.
I call it the sadness,
without heart feeling.
Yet it cannot feel,
neither can it see.
I thought it might grow,
yet it does not.

Inside I can feel a force,
so strong, it holds me up.
I look down,
I see horrors beyond my belief.

Chantelle Lowe

Yet when my eyes soar upwards,
they set upon beauty so deep,
it covers my soul.
The tips of the ends of my body,
can reach neither one nor the other.
But it serves me no purpose,
for they are not mine,
and I do not see them.

I close my eyes,
I can feel it calling,
but I will not go.
I WILL NOT GO!
It pulls me so tightly,
squashes my breath,
My ideas grow vague,
I can feel them slipping.
NO!
I feel myself gripping them,
unwilling to be lost,
unwilling to give in.

I hold my head up high,
I see the two worlds,

Chantelle Lowe

facing me side by side.
I hear them both calling,
and I feel the tears fall off my cheeks.
No longer can they hold me,
they are too far away,
yet I hear their whispers,
fleeting past,
and through. No, not through.
I try to block them out,
I try so hard.

I see my body fall,
so timid, so fragile.
I look beyond,
I see the hope die.
I see the gratitude,
of the ominous forces,
and I know I could've made it.
Yet I was so small, just one,
when there were so many others.
I want to stand strong,
I hold my body up,
it has found peace.

Chantelle Lowe

To think

Who would you think
would do such a thing?
Who would you think
would have the power to.

To turn

It is a supplement only,
to turn in on yourself,
and expose the pressures which hold,
then release.

Chantelle Lowe

To wake up

In the heavens of time I wake up,
it scolds me,
too finely, too delicately,
and far too accurate.
I am here, I am finally here,
in this place I have come to know,
but it is cold.
I must seek a new place,
somewhere kinder,
where I can stay in peace,
with hope of renewing my destiny.
Later on,
I will be warm and gentle,
yet I will be ever careful,
and ever cautious to show who I am.
For here,
I will hold myself strong,

Chantelle Lowe

in place by time and keep,
but what if it falls, so slowly,
that I do not notice, what is happening?
Yet I find I will remain out of reach,
from that which I have proven,
does not by any means, nor sincerity,
nor realistically, nor openly in any other manner,
exist.

Chantelle Lowe

Toward uncertainty

Time unfolds
and links itself to me.
Why did it call?
Too early and yet too late.
Playing on my thoughts,
calling towards uncertainty.
In a phrase,
I do not know.
But time seeps,
it lays it's hand,
then comes to rest.
No reason,
No room for indecision.
Just a space,
emptying forth.
Waiting,
not yet knowing,

Chantelle Lowe

that the seeds of essence
have run out.

Chantelle Lowe

To write

Oh my,
Where do I sit?
All day,
grasping the pen,
of truth.

Chantelle Lowe

Transfixation

To be the child I only see,
is a horrible transfixation.
Nonetheless, I do not see.
Horrible as it might seem,
I wish all would be
as it were.

Treasured thought

I see the break of dawn coming towards me,
in a ray of overwhelming light.
It seeps through my sorrowful night,
and calms me,
for the time I will need to be,
with the other.
Though in my mind I again smother,
that lone and treasure full thought.
For I have always considered myself the way I ought,
to be.

Chantelle Lowe

Two trees

In the middle of the night if I see it to be right,
I see branches reaching up and overlapping each other.
I see they belong to two trees, I am lying in the middle of them.
I stare up and wonder how they could live together and be so calm,
so peaceful and quiet, I can see their branches overlapping,
And wonder why they do not hurt each other, I cry.
I am lost from the outside world, it cannot hear me,
my comfort is the peace of those two trees and looking up to the stars,
until the cold comes and penetrates my sadness, my loss.
I have lost those two trees, I had to leave them behind,
if I look deep within me I can see the stars and the overlapping branches,
I can feel the two trees calling out to me, they are my only guardians.

Chantelle Lowe

Unattainable

Temporary status of decline,
in a way unimaginable.
It inhabits what is, in the moment of time.
Dysfunctional as it is, inescapable in its prime.
Terrifying to a result, as the issues role forth.
Time, the healer of displacement,
as it were in its way.
Discovery of old, recreation of new.
This is destruction of what was unattainable,
placed in unification.

Chantelle Lowe

Uncertainty

Nothing is as it was, I hate it,
I don't know what to make of it.
It is uncertain,
very uncertain, but then again it makes sense,
or the underlying tone does anyway.
Which isn't fair, well hardly at all,
I guess I must be used to it,
but can't see what that can achieve.

Chantelle Lowe

Underlying tone

When I was your age, young and rare,
I used to sit upon a tide,
and glimpse upon the future, dare,
you to see the break and find.

Its monstrous being compelled within,
do you see its dull sunken eyes,
and the pressing ageless of its sorrowed grin?
Dare mingle with this creature and compromise.

You would find its smirk so shallow,
and belie to you its untold wrath,
below, for its heart is hollow,
but will you find its underlying tone it has?

For deep beneath the surface it is corrupt,
beyond any extreme, and will never give it up.

Chantelle Lowe

Underneath the stains

Take away the pain and hurt which crease through my veins,
for all I know is all that has been in the gloom of yesterday,
no one hears, what no one sees underneath the stains.

Chantelle Lowe

Voice

I try,
I cannot remember,
what past lay behind me.

I fear,
I do not belong,
here or anywhere else.

I am,
not anything else,
but what you see before you.

I know,
all that I do not forget,
that I have heard of.

I seek,

Chantelle Lowe

not ever loneliness,
just what ever friendship I have.

I obey,
not your words,
only what I decide to do.

I listen,
for not my own voice,
but for others around me.

I take,
not what I don't want,
just what I need or like.

My own voice
is my most powerful possession.

My writing,
shows my thought.

Your ignorance,
is what can break me.

Chantelle Lowe

Your words,
can build or destroy me.

Whatever may happen,
you will still be here.

Chantelle Lowe

Wanting to disappear

Biding my time away from the world,
not knowing which way to turn.
In some ways I have already been hurled,
away from this place without concern.

There was no way I could fit in here,
when people turned the other way.
Like a shadow I wanted to disappear,
from the suffering brought through the day.

An image silhouetted on my mind,
crushing determination from within.
Cold tones being all that I can find,
in between the expectancy to begin.

I did not want it to be up to me,
to have to make the hard decisions.

Chantelle Lowe

But then I knew it had to be,
with all the searing premonitions.

Somehow I had known back in my first year,
that this would come to take its toll.

Chantelle Lowe

Went unnoticed

The time that passed this transition was immense,
calling forth on a rhythmless tide.
The feeling of trying to find what was lost,
something that went away unnoticed,
and now I do not know it.
A fathomless pit of information,
but do I need it?
I sigh, not knowing
whether going forward
is worse than going backward.

Chantelle Lowe

What I had

Why did I loose what I had,
when what I had,
was so little.

Chantelle Lowe

What to become

Who am I?
What am I?
What have I become?
I want to know,
but nobody will tell me.

Chantelle Lowe

What was

To become what is not,
then take it away,
and be left with what was.

Chantelle Lowe

When all is lost

When all is lost,
behind my wall of imaginary emotion.
I come against something so hard and solid,
it slices into my skin and embeds itself deep in my unloving arms,
I raise it high above my head and worship it.
As though it were a god,
the only god,
I ever knew or have known.
It places itself by my side,
warm and soft,
it delivers me from comfort.
Though,
behind its unsteady surface,
is a light,
shimmering and dull.
I want to touch it,
reach it.

But it is too precious,
I will rip it,
destroy it.
So I hold it,
enclose it,
empty my mind and rest my body.
Then lower my head,
down to its unearthing touch.
Its power,
its presence envelopes me.
I slowly fall,
and grow heavy,
my slow disturbed breathing is coming from faraway.
It is as though,
if I imagine
I am reaching my hand I can feel the edges of it,
with my numbed finger tips,
it is warm and moist.
In my eyes I see the black stream of its' cold touch swirling,
up against my time.
It is a creature,
or at least,
I can feel its senses,
fraying into my mind,

Chantelle Lowe

seeping into my thoughts,
calming them,
destroying them,
silently.

Chantelle Lowe

Where nothing is real

Please help me to understand,
in a world where nothing is real,
and hatred runs free.
In a place where carelessness devours the weak,
and lets the cruel reign.
This place is somewhere I do not wish to belong,
I do not see myself as being part of it,
even though I am strongly affected by it.
I want to be let free,
I want to be who I am,
I am like a stranger to this world,
I am apart from it,
when I see those around me.
It eats away at me,
yet I do not want to be like some.
I do not want to be friends
with those who hate.

Chantelle Lowe

They have nothing to give but hate,
and how will I grow with hate?

Who I am

All is abrupt as time stops,
here I am me.
Here is the world as I see it,
a collaboration.
This is the world I make it,
but what is it?
When I am still finding out who I am.

Chantelle Lowe

Wildest dreams

In a time long forgotten I stand,
always hoping, never holding back.
I want to be the person,
that pursues their wildest of dreams,
and conquers them.
I want to feel at peace with myself,
to be whole again,
as I once was.
This is not fear,
this is not anxiety,
this is letting your soul fly free,
and feel how it is to live,
in the moments that counts.
That in itself is important.

Chantelle Lowe

With a threat

With a threat upon my shoulders I haste less,
for I see no worthiness in it.
If only once I were to know,
myself be doing a worthy cause,
one of gratitude,
I'd feel it upon my shoulders,
to do in happiness.
Although I know this forgetful mind I carry,
does not serve me well,
and do thank a reminder,
though the rest leave up to me,
for I do set my time.

Without

Disillusionment conquers the soul,
as everything is made whole,
in the terms of the bottomless pit.

Extravagant is the destiny,
of those who wish to let it be,
without the satisfaction of it.

World of expectation

Time is more confusing than it is real.
I do not understand this world above,
which chooses to take advantage of me.
What is it that I have done,
In this world when I am but one.
I did not ask for this which came,
it was taken from me and now I am left to blame.
Did I have a say in this, I know not,
the choice was taken from my hands and into another's.
It seems I do not live up to normality,
for being normal is not something I am.
Give me space to grow and learn,
but I am still different in this world of expectation.
What made me so surreal,
I do not think that I understand.
My life was different
when I was too young to understand.

Chantelle Lowe

Now I am faced with the terms of this difference,
which haunt me in this world.
I cannot make sense of what I see,
in the same way as others.
I have been created to see differently,
and in this world what I am causes problems.
In areas above other people I am talented,
yet my grasping on basic understanding is vague.
I was not born into normality,
my voice was not accepted among others.
Still I stand alone,
creating my own path,
in this world of too many expectations.

Worthless

Were I not to ponder you I would think you dead,
how I have cried out in untold pain that is never to heal,
and you have abashed it, ignored it, it is worthless to you.

Through the years I have slept in the sorrow you have left behind,
it wraps itself around my body engulfing my head,
I cannot see for I am blind to it.
Every now and then when my frame gives way it peers its head,
and reveals as much as it can,
I detest it,
though there is no way of getting rid of it.
I find it hard to hold together with its ever waiting pace just below,
it's not dormant, how can it be dormant while I can feel its presence,
I want to slam it shut behind a door and hope it disappears but it won't,
I know it won't.

9 780648 778646